CREATIVE GARDEN LIGHTING

TIMBER PRESS

CREATIVE GARDEN LIGHTING

MICHÈLE OSBORNE

PHOTOGRAPHY BY STEVEN WOOSTER

to Charlotte for her constant
and loving presence

Published in North America in 2005 by
Timber Press, Inc.
The Haseltine Building
133 S.W. Second Avenue, Suite 450
Portland, Oregon 97204-3527, U.S.A.
www.timberpress.com

ISBN 0-88192-742-2

While all reasonable care has been taken during the
preparation of this edition, neither the publisher,
editors, nor the authors can accept responsibility for
any consequences arising from the use thereof or
from the information contained therein.

Commissioning Editor: Michèle Byam
Executive Art Editor: Sarah Rock
Designer: Miranda Harvey
Editor: Joanna Chisholm
Photography: Steven Wooster
Production: Gary Hayes
Index: Sue Farr

Set in Frutiger

Printed and bound in Hong Kong by
Toppan Printing Company Limited

INTRODUCTION

PREVIOUS PAGES The illuminated trunks of these two majestic olive trees rise above dazzling waves of lavender in full bloom and frame a path into a French potager. In the failing light, they focus the eye on the planting as well as structures farther away.

LEFT The darkened silhouette of the landscape seems to melt away against the mesmerizing shades of gold and intense purple within this grandiose sunset.

As the sky turns a deeper shade of violet, the golden glow of various copper fittings dotted around this garden prolongs the effect of the setting sun before playing a part in bringing life to the garden after dark. Columns of light then appear on the building, twig-lights twinkle in the carpets of box, recessed pathway lights lead to the attractively lit gazebo, and a single spike light draws the eye to the magnificent pompon pine in the foreground.

Gardens are so precious that we want to enjoy them all the time, not just on sunny days in the heat of summer. They have therefore often become an extension of the home, a refuge for relaxing or entertaining, whether in an urban or rural setting – and even after dark.

It is important to illuminate these reclaimed spaces. When doing this, it is essential to respect the natural components and soothing atmosphere inherently linked to a garden. The power of artificial light to make spaces look and feel glamorous as well as practical and safe has pushed the demand for a constantly expanding range of products. Originally, spotlights were used, but they were usually unattractive, provided a blinding light, and were so hot that they burnt any nearby plant. Only once beautiful Italian light fittings started to appear did garden designers feel encouraged to integrate lighting more fully into their schemes. With so many possibilities at their disposal, they felt free to look at gardens in dramatic terms and add the seduction of light to bucolic retreats or city hideouts.

This book is divided into three sections, in which an array of stunning gardens show: how lighting transforms and prolongs the use of a garden at night; what features and plants to highlight in order to create a magical scene; and the fittings best suited to achieve the desired effects, from neon to tiny spotlights.

This enclosed courtyard is separated from the house by only a glazed wall. Composed like an art installation, it forms a transition to the garden beyond. The light from a single uplighter focuses on a pebble mosaic panel and bounces off the polished concrete walls, bathing the space in an austere light perfectly in keeping with its uncompromising modernity. The huge shadows cast on the walls by the white moulded chairs add a monochrome decoration offset by the indigo sky. The darkened garden can be glimpsed through a slit in the wall.

This picture demonstrates perfectly how the light at dusk obliterates shadows and unifies tones. The main elements in this London garden all seem to radiate a pale purple glow before the various artificial lights come into full effect. The striking cantilevered pergola with its cedar timber uprights and stainless-steel crossbars has been fitted with downlighters for alfresco dining, while the architecture of the house is underlined by pillar wall lights to provide a striking backdrop for the topiary plants. Tapered zinc containers planted with majestic white agapanthus counterpoint the beautiful teak loungers poised just beyond the patio steps. These have been highlighted by small, evenly spaced LED lights so that they are safe for using at night-time.

The glow of sunset enhances the vibrant scarlet of this acer to perfection. In order to create a comparable visual feast when night has fallen, artificial lighting of this tree will be crucial, not only to do justice to its beauty but also to reinforce the sense of boundary at the end of this roof terrace.

The romantic mood conjured up while walking through a country garden at night under the moonlight or twinkling stars might seem difficult to surpass, yet a group of trees within the beam of a simple floodlight can create unexpected delight. Because the details of the branches are revealed, the shapes appear more majestic. Here, even the modest fennel with its yellow flowers and feathery leaves becomes a strong part of the composition. However, to avoid any risk of inappropriate levels of polluting illuminations garden lighting must be introduced with great sensitivity, particularly in the countryside.

All the glamour of lighting is represented here. This pool in the south of France is enchanting and could hardly be more inviting. The underwater lights make the night scene completely magical, as the blue mosaic sparkles and the mass of water seems utterly still and unreal. The row of ancient olive trees, each one lit from the base by a single spotlight, creates a stunning and reassuring visual barrier against the darkness beyond. The textured grey trunks and the silvery leaves are in full view and echo perfectly the gentle tones of the lavender closer to the pool and illuminated from a nearby tree.

As night falls on the financial district of Canary Wharf in London, numerous windows light up the distant tower blocks. Lights also come on in the oval swimming pool on the tenth floor of this residential block, making the grey mosaic shimmer. A single band of fibreoptic lighting in yellow underlines the top of the timber-clad service tower before continuing through a whole sequence of other colours. This simple scheme complements perfectly the very urban setting, giving just the right accent to this extraordinary terrace and allowing it to merge with the vast sky above.

Here, the same terrace is here lit up slightly earlier in the evening by the glorious gold, pink, and deep purple of the setting sun. The surface of the pool reflects this dazzling show like a mirror, as do the glazed walls of the skyscrapers beyond. One underwater light in the pool, still only barely visible in the fading daylight, is a harbinger of the illuminations still to come.

This is the private and intimate part of a garden where public functions take place. The ironwork pergola is deliberately plain, although it has been covered entirely by a grapevine to enhance the feeling of privacy. Tea-lights have been placed in glass jars so that they are protected from the wind. They not only form a centrepiece on the table but are also distributed on a small side table and – to define the space – on the bars of the pergola. A light bulb with its old-fashioned, white porcelain shade is placed above the kitchen door and supplies the illumination on the right of this scene. It is often switched off when meals have been served, to let the gentle glow of candles complement the softness of summer nights.

INTO THE NIGHT

This is the moment when a feeling of anticipation and glamour envelops the garden. The blazing sky slowly turns various shades of violet, and lights are switched on in preparation for the evening. In some gardens, a control panel inside the house triggers complex combinations of illuminations that create different atmospheres; in others, the owner may walk round with a remote control setting off various areas, depending on the desired mood or the latest acquisition to be displayed. Before guests arrive, candles can be lit to complete the picture.

PREVIOUS PAGES This garden has room for a wide range of activities after sunset. A covered area – brightly lit for comfortable dining – is framed by two giant palm trees lit from below to reveal the dramatic texture of their trunks. Pierced concrete screens punctuate the whole space and are given great presence by pink and turquoise neon lights. Recessed lights guide nocturnal users first to a pale blue plunge pool and then onto a dark blue swimming pool.

At nightfall, this wonderful roof terrace in Queens, New York, is prepared for the evening. The festoons of lights dotted on the vast Queensborough Bridge have just come on, and the lights of Manhattan are starting to glitter in the background. The roof terrace has been divided into several well-proportioned areas, all paved with textured concrete slabs, and a central fountain is set among black pebbles and slate. Richly planted containers and a wooden

pergola further define the space. All the different lights on the terrace have been switched on ready for a dinner party, but in this moment of fading light, when a grey haze seems to envelop everything, their full effect is still only to be guessed at.

Now that the sky is darker, the lights can truly shine out. In the sitting area, small uplighters in the planters accentuate the shape of shrubs and their lush underplanting. Spotlights focus the eye on the striking fountain planted with papyrus, enhancing the texture of the concrete paving. Meanwhile, the soft glow of candles seems to be everywhere – in storm lamps, in little candlesticks with shades, and in metal lanterns – making the space even more inviting for the owners and their guests. This terrace has been carefully designed for use through the day and night. What makes it truly remarkable, though, is how the lighting has been cleverly designed to link the intimate setting to the potentially overpowering urban backdrop of industrial chimneys, gigantic bridge, and numerous skyscrapers.

In daylight, this roof terrace in Tribeca, New York, reveals its impressive, clean design. The pale decking with its inset of dark slate is a perfect foil for the modern furniture and its crisp white cushions. The timber containers along the parapet walls are painted rich brown and planted with birches and pristine stachys, foxgloves, and grasses at their feet. Buddleias and cornus against the building complete the picture. A large BBQ gleams at one end, and the Hudson River shimmers beyond it.

PREVIOUS PAGES All lights are blazing here, inside and outside, in perfect harmony to conjure this theatrical effect when the owners of the house are entertaining. The owners' brief to the designer was to create a formally classical garden; it had to be robust enough to balance the conflicting aims of making the house look imposing and the garden ready for a lot of entertaining all year round, while at the same time accommodating the needs of five young children. Pillar lights on the building accentuate the architecture as well as illuminate the dining terrace. Copper "eyelids" light up the steps, and twig-lights outline the formal planting, while tiny underwater bulbs reveal 11 small jets in a square pool near the conservatory.

Night has now fallen on the same terrace. The lighting brings a sense of privacy and comfort to a space that could easily feel exposed. Little spotlights placed in the planters pick out the row of tall birches opposite the apartment, and create a visual barrier and the feeling of a garden. Long tubes fitted with light bulbs hang in the trees, throwing tiny shards of light through star-shaped perforations. Directional lights fixed to the building set the sitting and dining areas firmly in focus. Bespoke wall sconces act as reflectors to enhance the planting against the building, while diffused interior lighting adds an atmospheric glow. The end of the terrace has been left open, so that the lights of the city become part of the décor.

The pleasure of being outside no longer has to end as soon as the sun goes down. That wonderful feeling of wellbeing and mystery associated with warm nights can now be enjoyed in comfort, thanks to the constantly improving design of weather-proof furniture and – most of all – to the vast range of lighting devices and systems available to garden designers and owners. Whether you want to spend more time in the garden to entertain guests, have a family meal, simply enjoy the stillness of the night, or have a swim at midnight, all is now possible.

The space reserved for eating in this garden is close to the house and sheltered by a dark woven-sail roof. For alfresco meals, the lighting comprises wall lights fixed to the building and their reflection off the white walls. The internal lighting adds a gentle glow, which is enhanced by the Christmas-tree decorations seen through the glazed door and revealing that this evening summer scene was photographed in the southern hemisphere.

It is difficult to imagine a better way than this to transform a tiny sunken space at the bottom of a tall New York building. One wall of the building was taken down over two floors and replaced by huge panes of glass. At the same time an area was scooped out on the ground floor to create a small raised terrace above a tiny courtyard. The wall of the facing building is of patterned concrete painted white to bring in more light. It has now become a giant artwork to be viewed from the living area inside. Bands of highly polished aluminium are fixed to the wall to reflect the sky during the day as well as lights at night, while strips of pink, yellow, and purple Perspex provide the only colour in this monochrome composition. At night, a complex sequence of commands puts in motion a never-ending, mesmerizing light show illuminating and bouncing off the various materials to distract from the potentially oppressive height of the walls and prolong the enjoyment of this extraordinary space.

entertaining, dining

For many people, dining outside used to be something experienced on holiday in a hot country and fondly remembered. Now, however, it is becoming more prevalent, thanks to a greater awareness of the outdoor and the increasing accessibility of a whole range of lifestyle products – from parasols to gas heaters. When well furnished, a terrace or patio is often a place of choice to entertain, especially when it includes the added magic of a well-thought out lighting scheme. This can concentrate on the dining area, invite guests on a nocturnal walk, or highlight an attractive vista. Table illuminations should ideally combine downlighters fixed to the house or the crossbars of a pergola, for comfortable light levels, with candles and possibly fairy lights coiled round a parasol for atmosphere.

The lighting in this elegant courtyard could not be simpler yet it works perfectly because of the precise design. Symmetry reigns: tall clay pots with box balls are lined up in strict formation on either side of small round lights set in black marble pebbles, while square fittings illuminate the bronze finish on the plaster panels. The teak dining table with its striking setting is lit only by tiny candles.

After a dinner alfresco on a chilly night, this summer room is particularly inviting. Built across the whole width of a small London garden, the room could have been intrusive, but, instead has been cleverly integrated by rhythmic lighting along both walls leading to it. The area has been given presence by the playful strip of light under the raised platform.

This solidly constructed gazebo with its tiled roof and brick pillars has been conceived as an outdoor dining room. The specially designed copper candelabra with its pointed bulbs brings instant glamour while providing excellent light above the dining table. The recessed pathway lights at the base of each pillar define the space with just the right amount of reflection on the surrounding plants, like the horsetail with its graphic lines, to create a soft transition with the darkness beyond.

As it is constructed on two levels, this relatively small London terrace might have been a difficult space to use effectively. However, the uncompromising design has transformed it into a very elegant outdoor room with separate areas for nocturnal activities. The tall geometric clay pots with their square cushions of box are the core of the design and are cleverly accentuated by recessed uplighters in the teak decking. On the lower level the pots form a dividing colonnade, and on the upper terrace the pots' shadows are projected onto the top of the wall in regular geometric patterns.

This roof terrace in New York is so self-
contained that there is no feeling of being
overlooked by the many tall buildings around.
The copper planters are the main feature here.
Not only do they give unity and define different
areas with trees and masses of colourful
seasonal planting, but their reflective quality is
also a huge asset and has been used with great
ingenuity. The illumination from the spotlights
buried in the planters or fixed to the building
walls washes over the copper at just the right
level around the sitting and dining areas.
Candles in a tall storm lamp and small glass jars
provide a note of intimacy at the dining table.

relaxing, swimming

Gardens have always played their part in helping people rest their bodies and heal their souls, whether through tending plants, reading in a deck chair, or just sitting still. Now that pools appear in many more gardens regardless of the climate, swimming too has become a popular garden activity. Lighting can greatly help to create a soothing atmosphere around the pool, although a delicate balance has to be found as too much light would destroy the magic but too little could be impractical or even dangerous. In early evening, lighting could be strong, to direct guests to the swimming area, whereas later, when all are safely seated beside the pool, the glow of candles might suffice. It is essential that the route to a swimming pool and its perimeter is clearly indicated, and the water itself must be properly lit not only for a stunning visual effect but also for safety reasons.

The powerful recessed spotlight illuminating the terrace of this ancient property could create a blinding and unpleasant effect. Instead, the wonderful texture of the pale stone wall seems to absorb the light, while the vast white umbrella diffuses it and provides a radiant roof to the dining area flanked by orange trees in green glazed pots. This type of projected light works well here because of the scale of the building, but it can easily be adapted with a smaller fitting to warm up the walls of an urban garden terrace.

The intimate seating corner of this London roof garden has two sources of built-in lighting. The perfectly shaped acer is lit from below by a fitting hidden behind the clay container, and this creates a boundary against the open space beyond. A downlighter fixed to the building is directed towards the two metal cubes, to reflect and spread the light. For more intimacy, shallow metal bowls have been filled with tea-lights.

The owners of this garden outside London wanted the swimming area to be totally self-contained and safe, so that it could be enjoyed well into the night. The underwater lighting illuminates the pale blue mosaic of the pool, accentuating the dark lines on the steps. The summerhouse flanked by both pergolas and small buildings is lit internally with such flair that it forms the focal point of the scene. A chandelier hung from the ceiling above the dining table is complemented by a row of uplighters hidden in the roof, making the warm yellow of the interior walls glow against the pale grey of the external walls. The stained-glass windows decorating the end building – the one seen here houses a changing room and small kitchen – are also lit from inside, and are reflected in the pool for further effect. Downlighters fixed to the pergola accentuate its shape and show the way, but leave the hammock in restful darkness. Even the moon adds its glow on this particular night.

The lighting designer of this Kentish garden in the south of England believes ardently that spike spots are the most effective way of illuminating plants and trees. He demonstrates here how he has created an intimate context for the pale blue mass of the lit-up swimming pool, with a few counterpoints of lights. The delicate tracery of *Verbena bonariensis* in the foreground creates a visual barrier, while the majestic cedars located at the far end are lit from the base to form a more solid screen. To show off the pale stone of the newly restored enclosing wall, a lawn light has been placed at the base among the planting, while lights recessed into the flanking walls transform the steps into a sculptural element.

This lap pool occupies a raised area at one end
of a New York roof terrace. Although protected
on two sides by walls, it is overlooked on
another side by very tall buildings. The aim of
the lighting here, therefore, is to provide a safe
but discreet environment when using the pool
at night. Underwater lights simply throw beams
onto the shallow floor and the sides of the pool.

A successful garden, however big or small, does not reveal itself all at once. It creates surprises by playing visual tricks with perspective, planting, surfaces, or cleverly positioned ornaments. Lighting, too, can provide designers with another whole range of creative tricks, enabling them to reinforce a scheme or enhance a feature such as a fountain or sculpture. They can also conjure up different spatial arrangements by concentrating light on one area and leaving another totally in the dark, then highlighting an object farther away to confuse the sense of scale.

To enter this suburban house in Auckland, New Zealand, you need to go through the most extraordinary front garden. Its uncompromising design is a source of inspiration and provides a great contrast to the neighbouring houses with their red roofs and net curtains, which could belong to the suburb of any city. Many of the elements in this garden would fit any contemporary garden. Great slabs of concrete with a matt silver finish mark the entrance and screen the house from the road. More disconcertingly, the front door is reached by crossing a pool of water. It almost feels as if only the brave should tread here. In the water is a solitary female figure lying on her back.

At night the whole garden is transformed, as if by magic, while an incredible drama unfolds. The purpose of this space now seems to matter very little, because lighting it in such a spectacular fashion gives it a dream-like quality. A whole network of underwater fibreoptic lights is set on an automatic timer so that every 15 seconds they switch between red, green, blue, and, finally, white, to bring the viewer back to reality. Bathed in a golden glow, the spotlit figure appears radiant. The silver walls reflect the indoor lighting and now seem to be made of burnished gold, while a sheet of water flows from a slit in one of the walls and falls over a line of tiny lights.

The whole atmosphere has been altered yet again. The lighting timer has been stopped so that the abstract quality of the composition can now be fully observed. Part of the pool is washed in the richest red, which seems to bleed into a pure blue pigment. The naked figure has assumed a disquieting quality: the truncated limbs seem more meaningful in this red pool, and the head – thrown back into a blue shadow – now appears to be in anguish. The perforated metal bridge glimmers starkly to reinforce the hardness of the image, evoking fire and maybe some impending gloom. Although this might seem a strange design for the front garden of a suburban house, in fact it illustrates perfectly how an outside space can be much more than a place in which to display plants, by showing how innovative lighting can help create a showcase for art.

visual delights

As it is now possible to devise extremely complicated lighting schemes, the opportunities to create something wonderful and pleasing are almost infinite. Lighting a garden after dark no longer involves shining a spotlight on one or two plants as an afterthought; instead, it means almost staging a play by adding drama and excitement to the garden, as well as creating a feast for the eyes. The garden becomes a complete environment in which to be charmed, amazed, and maybe also slightly disorientated – like watching fireworks or gazing at the stars on a clear night. When the visitor walks along a path to the end of the garden, some groups of plants may be revealed in great detail against the black mass of hedges. In other gardens, lights can be placed high up in a tree, to create moon-like shadows to step over on the ground. When the eye looks back towards the illuminated house, the diffused glow from inside adds a pleasant feeling of cohesion between the indoor and outdoor environments. This sense of wonder can also be felt from inside when looking out onto a small courtyard or a terrace in which a range of effects using various colours, intensity, and reflections can transform the space in front of the windows into a permanent art installation.

The purpose of lighting this carefully designed garden, which here glistens in the rain, is to provoke a sense of disorientation. Spotlights have been placed with precision so that they reinforce this feeling and highlight crucial elements within the garden. They are set, for example, at the base of the immaculately tied bamboo fence, at the foot of the beautifully shaped acer, and across the path so that the pieces of chiselled granite and the bamboo fountain are delineated, as well as being set into the steps to lead the eye on beyond the stone path. The design is so still and confident that it is surprising that this garden is in London rather than Japan.

PREVIOUS PAGES Lighting has transformed this small sunken space between tall buildings into a work of abstract art. Downlighters fixed to the building are programmed to create an ever-changing show, in turn illuminating the texture of the concrete wall, bouncing off the strips of coloured Perspex, or making the bands of polished metal gleam like mirrors. The pale pebbles spread over the ground between strips of metal – so that they brighten the space even more – have taken on a sculptural quality under the power of the light beams.

Is this scene inside or outside? The feature on the right, reminiscent of a display window in a museum, is eerily lit by a neon strip fixed to the concrete opening, while spotlights within the space highlight the plants. The strongly lit single jar further blurs the separation between house and garden, as it appears to continue the line of pots displayed inside, by the window.

In this extraordinary succession of openings, simple white lights have been used to illuminate walls painted in different shades of blue, to form a totally abstract composition. The reflection of the sky and the silvery astelia in the still water further adds to the feeling of disorientation.

PREVIOUS PAGES The lighting here is almost theatrical in its effects. The imposing towers of this French château are lit by powerful spotlights, to create a fantastic golden backdrop to the potager in the foreground. This retains an intimate scale, thanks to its own sensitive lighting. Each pillar of the rose pergola is lit upwards not only to highlight the plants but also to emphasize the roof above the central fountain and the raised crown of the structure.

RIGHT Mirrors are often used in gardens to generate the illusion of a bigger space. Here, a mirror framed by trellis is fixed to a building overlooking a roof terrace. At night the visual trick works to its full effect. Whatever is beyond the terrace remains in darkness, while the layers of shrubs and trees are fully lit, making it difficult to know exactly how the space is organized and certainly making it seem mysterious. The wall lights on the parapet define the boundary with their strong architectural shape, yet they also give out a strikingly diffused light.

Lighting schemes do not have to be complicated in order to conjure up an enchanting scene. In this country garden in Surrey, England, the area shown here is farthest from the house and is reached by a long walk down a very steep hill. By positioning lights judiciously, this small flat clearing, which could have been disappointing after the powerful drama of the descent has been transformed into an enticingly bucolic space. In fact it is lit mainly by a single powerful spotlight. The shadows of grasses make dramatic shapes on the lawn, while all the illuminated surrounding vegetation accentuates the feeling of seclusion. Two more spotlights in the centre hint at the small pond concealed among the foliage.

When a small courtyard is such an integral part of the house it is important that both relate to each other, as has been achieved here using lighting. The glass balustrade reflects the blue LED lights inside the house and seems to project them into the garden to integrate it perfectly. Other complementary elements of the lighting design are: the golden glow of the spotlit back wall; the rill and its spout also spotlit but at different intervals to the wall; the tall Moroccan lanterns forming another line of gentle light; the candle reflected into a pure circle of gold above the rill spout; and the eccentric candelabra surrounding a cactus. Finally, the reflections in the dark, polished concrete floor give this courtyard a totally enchanting atmosphere.

STAGING THE ILLUSION

PREVIOUS PAGES This is a perfect example of how a utilitarian and well-tried light fitting can produce the most unexpected effect. A narrow trench at the base of the boundary wall has been filled with drainage material and upside-down lengths of drainage channels overlaid with strips of waterproof fluorescent tubes. The resulting harsh light not only enhances the texture of the wall and some of the trees but also obliterates what is beyond its range.

Designing a successful lighting scheme with well-planned illuminations can be compared to stage lighting, because the positioning of the lights involves artistic sensibility and creativity, whether the layout is integral to the design of a new garden or a whole system is added to an established one. This book has already explained how lighting can be used to strengthen a scheme and delight the senses. Now it will suggest ways to illuminate paths in a darkened garden at the same time as focusing attention and enhancing particular features such as fountains, rills or pools, plants or trees, and ornaments such as sculptures and statues.

Two forms of lighting are combined here to make a very striking impact: the blue light from a neon strip fixed to the concrete beam; and the white light of a spotlight behind the pillar. These bathe the white concrete walls in a purple haze that is in perfect harmony with the grey tone of the spectacular agaves.

RIGHT Gabions backed by blue Perspex are lit from behind to form an extraordinary "floating" wall at the end of a garden. On a rainy day, the reflections on the wet slate path add a further surreal element. The only hint that this scene occurs in a garden is the presence of the lamium planted on either side of the path.

showing the way

To enjoy a garden after sunset, it is important to be able to move around easily without a feeling of impending danger at every turn. Forgetting for a moment glamour and mystery, this is where lighting plays its most basic and crucial role. A line of tea-lights in glass jars might prove a festive and efficient solution to guide guests to a celebration dinner, but, if the outdoor space is part of family life in summer, a more permanent system should be installed.

Routes from the house to various parts of the garden might include paths of different textures and materials, bridges or stepping stones, and at least one change of level. It is essential to light these efficiently and safely. If fittings are recessed in the floor finish, they must be flush with the ground to avoid tripping, and be fitted with anti-glare screens. To highlight steps, use "eyelid" fittings to concentrate the light downwards, and lights recessed in the flank walls to send beams sideways onto the treads. Along paths, thin stainless-steel bollards give a pleasant diffused light; in a more traditional garden, copper fittings spreading the light downwards under a "mushroom" top might be more in keeping.

"Eyelid" lights recessed into the low concrete wall illuminate these limestone steps without blinding the users. They also make the landing inviting for those wishing to recline on the white fabric chairs before going down to the nearby pool or watching swimmers in it. Only a fraction of the wide staircase is shown here, which explains the seemingly disconcerting placement of the loungers at the top of the stairs.

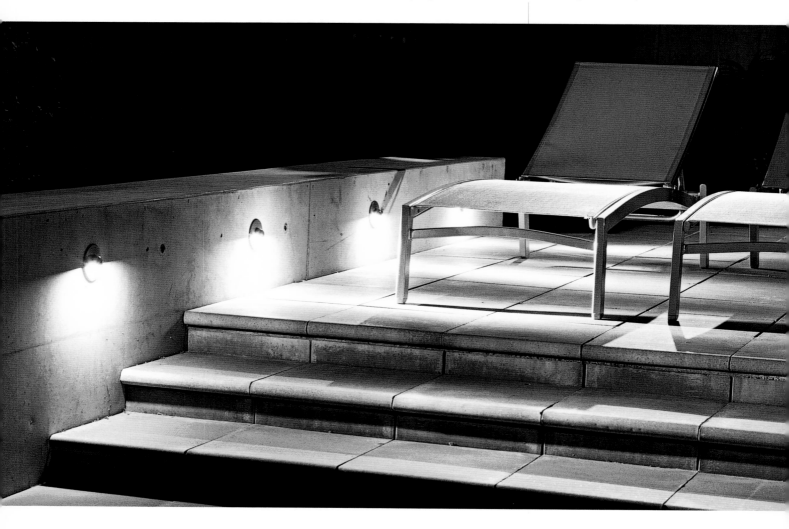

The handrail of this beautifully detailed timber staircase linking the road entrance to the garden plays its role perfectly. An integral part of the stainless-steel rail are the strip lights illuminating the steps and the bottom of the timber-clad wall. The top of the wall is left in shadow above a sharp bright line, which emphasizes the route of the stairs.

LEFT and RIGHT It is interesting to compare the totally different ways in which these two timber bridges have been lit, both reflective of their functions.

The one on the left spans a sunken garden in order to link an orchard to a potager. The minimal lighting is in harmony with the gentle atmosphere. A simple rope light has been fixed to the underside of the bridge, safely guiding users across the bridge as well as generating a light effect of its own through the slats.

The bridge seen on the right crosses over a shallow channel of water. Originally this example was designed for a public project at Canary Wharf, London, by a team of architects and lighting designers. It has now, however, been developed as a standard commercial product. To ensure that the elegant lines of the bridge were free of any fittings, strip lights were incorporated into the top of the balustrade on one side and angled to provide sufficient lighting levels across the bridge, making it safe and inviting to cross at night.

LEFT In this London garden, the lighting scheme is so well integrated into the elegant design that it adds a strong rhythm to the composition as well as emphasizing different areas and individual features. All recessed, the fittings are set in white gravel and light up the row of multistemmed amelanchiers and also funnel attention towards a sitting area. There, further uplighters between pots mark out the end wall of the garden. Other uplighters are placed between low box hedging, where they illuminate the carved-oak sculptures and bring light to the top of the teak fence, for a greater sense of privacy. The eight jets springing from a limestone platform are each lit by a fibreoptic bullet, while all routes to and from the house are indicated by small recessed wall lights.

Here, blister lights set into the flank walls of shallow limestone steps lead the visitor onto a timber deck. This surrounds a swimming pool situated behind the glazed doors just visible on the right of the picture. The golden glow of halogen lights engenders a glamorous and inviting atmosphere that is wholly in keeping with the beautiful loungers and the spotlit zinc containers filled with espaliered apple trees at the back of the deck.

RIGHT The owners of this London garden wanted the illuminated spire of an adjacent church to form part of their landscape at night. The designer therefore orchestrated two lines of light to balance out the tower: white LEDs set in the steps and uplighters enhancing the standing stone and bamboos; and softer halogen lights transforming the deck into a stage by lighting the parapet wall and the glass fin above it. Such a well-thought out scheme has transformed a potentially overpowering "borrowed" feature into a distinct asset.

This path of concrete stepping stones set in pebbles leads from the house to a summer room at the end of the garden. Between it and a boundary wall are bamboo plants punctuated by simple spotlights encased in rubber and spiked into the ground at regular intervals. There is no attempt to conceal the black flexes of the spotlights, so they and the black bamboo stems leave dark lines among the pebbles.

A long, meandering path follows the contours of this garden terraced on a steep hill and leads to a flat area with a small pond at the farthest end. Nocturnal walks could be hazardous in such country areas, which are very dark at night. Light levels should be strong enough to ensure safety without overwhelming the garden and transforming it into a landing pad. Egg-shaped downlighters, each fitted with a black plastic hood, have here been screwed onto lengths of vertical railway sleepers at the correct height to indicate changes of level or direction along the path. Their robust design is perfectly in keeping with the general atmosphere in the garden.

This orange tree in a green-glazed Montpellier pot at the end of the path is one of four positioned around a stone basin in this vegetable garden. The wonderful texture of the paving is due to a traditional method of laying small tapered stone cubes closely together. It is fully emphasized by simple spotlights spiked into the ground along the rows of fruit trees, which are trained in cordons on either side. As the trees are pruned to a height of 1.5m (5ft), the lighting is kept at a deliberately low level, creating an attractively marked route.

water transformed

Water and light have long been eye-catching partners. Whether water is rippling, splashing, or cascading, it is transformed by light as it refracts through millions of droplets to create tiny strands, scintillating stars, or the illusion of a solid mass, to the endless fascination of the onlooker. Waterworks in the grand manner, as in France or Italy, would be lit up by torches to produce grandiose spectacles for the pleasure of monarchs and dignitaries. Nowadays, such vast displays, as at Versailles, France, are lit by electricity and orchestrated for the enjoyment of the public, yet their magic is enduring.

Fountains recently introduced into public spaces often provide interactive features, in which children delight in running between jets unexpectedly springing from a paved area. In the evening, these fountains are lit up, which adds to the playful element, particularly when the lights are programmed to follow a sequence of changing colours.

As is often the case, the design of public or corporate spaces serves as a laboratory for new ideas, which garden owners are then inspired to reproduce. This increases the demand for new products, thus water features, complete with underwater lights, have become almost compulsory elements of garden design. Results can vary considerably, but it is difficult to deny that, when successfully used, the calming power of water brings focus and harmony to a garden.

RIGHT A breathtaking effect is produced when an underwater light is placed precisely where water from a flat metal spout hits a rill. The water appears like liquid gold splattering into thousands of sparkling filaments against the still, dark mass of the rill. Such a setup as this demonstrates to perfection the benefits of combining light and water.

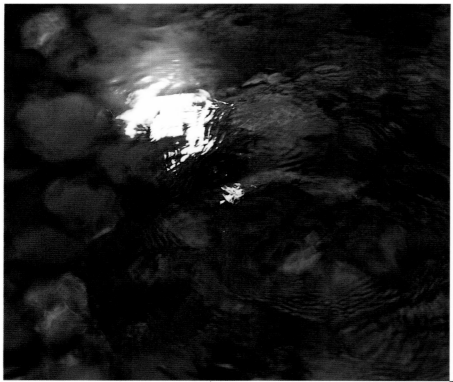

A nearby fountain splashes water onto the polished pebbles and glass chips spread on the floor of this urban courtyard. Such a magical combination of light and water clearly shows yet again how simple materials can be unexpectedly transformed. The wet pebbles are lit from above by downlighters fixed to the building, and each one reflects the light and sparkles like a precious stone.

The tiny underwater light shown here is one of a series marking the length of a 10m (30ft) rill lined with black pebbles in a contemporary garden. The use of underwater lighting in rills has transformed these traditional water features into stunning shafts of light cutting through a garden at night, to indicate a vista or bring drama to the landscape.

This tiny courtyard in New York has been designed to be viewed from inside the apartment, both at ground level and from above. It contains robust materials, some of which have been recycled from a previous use for the building. A small cascade juts out from a sitting area on the ground floor. The water flows along a length of cast-iron gutter into a basin excavated in the sunken courtyard and bridged by an industrial metal grille. A single wide-beamed spotlight placed under the basin not only draws attention to the movement of water in this very still space but also establishes lines of strong shadows on the mesh. These are in keeping with the overall feel, while at the same time highlighting the roundness of the pebbles.

It was important to light up the whole space in this large English country garden. Spike lights at the base of trees indicate the way from the house to the gazebo as well as enclosing the area. The level change near the house has been used to accommodate a cascade. A thin sheet of water slips over a shelf into a stainless-steel basin, and an underwater light maximizes reflections. In the top pool, a tiny spotlight enhances a conical planter filled with sedum.

This unusual water feature is 2m (6½ft) long and so makes a bold statement in the front garden of a London house. The slab of pure black granite facing the house is washed by water coming out of 19 holes at the top and then bubbling into a trough at the bottom. At night the scene is most impressive, as only the narrow water channel is brightly lit, leaving the stone slab in complete darkness.

LEFT Not every garden can accommodate a pool large enough for such waterworks, which illustrate wonderfully how lighting transforms the very texture of water. This is the first feature that visitors to this garden will encounter, so underwater spotlights have been dotted all around the pool and below the jets to create powerful illuminations. The huge volume of water projected by the tall jets is transformed to resemble a diaphanous cloth of gold.

This beautiful antique fountain set in the centre of a stone basin releases only the gentlest trickle of water from its carved top. During the day, the water from the fountain is hardly visible, apart from the slight ripples in the pool. Yet at night, when the strong underwater spotlights come on, the stone pier is lit from all sides, revealing the surrounding watery mass.

LEFT This extraordinary fountain made out of a huge recycled cog has been cleverly lit in order to give it centre stage. Spike lights in planters at low level and downlighters on the pergola beyond ensure that the papyrus-planted basin and its gentle jet are lit from all angles. The lighting is further reflected on the wet stones and on the shiny surface.

A line of fibreoptic lights just inside the spout of this metal arch transforms water into a solid mass as it falls into a circular stainless-steel pool. The palpable energy of the water is balanced by the soft lighting bouncing over the pebble mosaic by Maggy Howarth and the spike lights enhancing the rich planting.

Here, water flows from a slit in a wall clad in reclaimed Welsh slate. It then falls over a sheet of purple Perspex into a long trough edged with lead. At night, the underlit Perspex projects into the garden a purple glow, which combines with the pale green beam highlighting the striking shape of the prickly pears (*Opuntia robusta*) in the foreground.

RIGHT Garden and lighting designers working closely together have conceived this plot as a "moon garden" and have used a colour scheme of blues and whites for the planting and lighting. The granite-clad cube grooved on three sides but left natural at the front is a magnificent water feature at the centre of the design. The impact of the white foaming water gushing down the front face is enhanced by white underwater lighting shining upwards, while the sides remain dark. The white heads of the alliums, "floating" above a carpet of blue nepeta in the foreground, are caught in the beam of uplighters.

For the owners of this London garden, the pool, lined in dark Indian limestone, was a central element of the design, perfectly complementing the planting and the authentic Japanese fence built *in situ* out of bamboo, black twine, and charred timber posts. Working closely with their designer, they also recognized the crucial role of lighting not only in allowing them to enjoy the garden into the night but also to frame views and vistas from the house. They chose to highlight features and plants with great precision, playing with the reflective power of the still pool or the wet Norwegian pine decking when it gleams in the rain.

This beautiful grouping of white multistemmed birches (*Betula utilis*) underplanted with ferns and purple *Iris* 'Harriette Halloway' is given an eerie quality by the use of a blue dichroic filter dropped over a white spike light fitted with anti-glare louvres. This scheme works all the year round, as the blue haze bounces off the silky white trunks, but it is especially good when the irises are in bloom.

plants and trees

Plants are, of course, the essence of a garden but do they benefit from being put in the spotlight? Is their natural beauty enhanced by artificial means? These are very important questions, as garden owners increasingly want to extend the use of their outdoor space, and concurrently their interest in lighting grows.

Trees are obvious candidates for illumination. When lit from below, the shape, height, and texture of a trunk and the pattern of branches can be revealed and greatly enhanced with endless visual fascination. A light shining down from the top of a tree will achieve moonshine effects, with eerie shadows instantly producing an atmosphere of mystery in the garden. To give structure to the garden at night, position a spotlight on plants with bold overall shapes such as topiary or clipped hedges. Concentrate the beam mainly on strongly coloured plants and interestingly shaped leaves while keeping the effect discreet, so that the very nature of the garden is respected and light pollution is avoided.

RIGHT This extraordinary carpet of succulent plants – *Echeveria* 'Perle von Nürnberg', *Sempervivum ciliosum*, and haworthia – is served well by a simple spotlight because the sumptuous texture and strong pattern of each rosette is picked up and the jewel-like, red edge of the echeveria is allowed to sparkle. The small light fitting placed at ground level has been chosen to enhance the delicacy of the plants without being overbearing.

A single light has been recessed into the wooden deck so that it shines onto this simple planting scheme at night. The mass of pale purple petunias and white busy Lizzies (*Impatiens*) appears transfixed above the scallop of light shining on the "lead" surface of this fibreglass planter.

Within the profuse jungle of this garden, the lighting introduces an element of surprise while highlighting the best specimens. Here, the big leaves of a paulownia are underlit by a spotlight fitted with a green filter. Although such a colour choice might not seem obvious when leaves are to be enhanced, it does in fact work well in this site, as the beam is diffused by the dense planting; the light also catches the red flowers of a buddleia.

LEFT What could demonstrate more dramatically the role of lighting in a garden than this amazing composition? The fantastic sculptured shape of the New Zealand Christmas tree (*Metrosideros excelsa*) is reflected in the smooth surface of the infinity pool. The rather harsh white light of a large spotlight at the base of the trunk reveals every single branch and other fine details of this perfect tree. As if to give an idea of scale, the light beam encompasses a group of acanthus in full bloom, but leaves the sea just beyond the railings in complete darkness.

The twisted trunk of this ancient olive tree (*Olea europaea*) in a French potager is displayed here in all its rugged simplicity, and the tiny silvery leaves can be seen almost individually. The spotlight has been spiked in the ground 1m (3ft) away from the tree, among the lavender (*Lavandula angustifolia*), to provide a gentle glow as the light bounces off the purple flowers. This traditional planting combination is found all over the Mediterranean region.

This exuberant group of bright red and yellow Icelandic poppies (*Papaver nudicaule*) which are interspersed with the crimson pincushions of *Cirsium rivulare*, shows how strong colours respond best to lighting. The blue flowers of the catmint (*Nepeta racemosa* 'Walker's Low') are hardly visible, while the sharply cut-out leaves of a potentilla stand out in the foreground.

Here, the gentle atmosphere of the natural design has been respected, and only minor illuminations have been introduced. The lighting produces a secretive feel and distorts scale as it is directed towards a small pond below a large garden terraced on the side of a hill. The profuse summer planting provides an excellent cover for a strong spike light. Instead of lighting the wooden launch or the water directly, the light fitting has been placed off-centre so that it filters through the mass of polygonums, astilbes, and reeds (*Typha*), and grazes the oversized metal dragonflies hovering above the black surface of the pond.

LEFT This exotic group leading to and enveloping a sitting area has been lit by low-voltage halogen bulbs. These have been supplied with built-in glare guards and set in black fittings to "disappear" as much as possible, so that attention is directed on the magnificent tree fern and its entourage of bamboos and grasses.

When wandering down a long path in a country garden set on the side of a steep hill, interest is maintained by lighting groups of plants along the way. This is the end of summer, so the plants might not look their best, yet the intentions of the designer are clear. A wide beam spotlight fixed on the slope opposite washes each group in a golden glow to conjure a reassuring feeling against the darkened landscape and to display attractive specimens. In this instance, these are the palm *Trachycarpus fortunei*, a tree fern (*Dicksonia antarctica*), and the tall stems and purple flowers of *Verbena bonariensis*, as well as the red flowers of *Epimedium* x *rubrum*.

For the designers of this spectacular urban garden, the lighting was as important as the planting and hard landscaping. They planned an eight-circuit system activated by a hand-held remote control to highlight different features or, as here, to reveal everything at once and create an enchanting atmosphere. Blue light has been used to play on the water and reflections: for example, mint-blue fluorescent tubes have been positioned behind the vertical water feature and the recessed glass sheet; and LED strips underline the pool and the glass bridge. Low-voltage uplighters have been carefully placed to balance the blue lighting, and are concentrated mainly on the exotic planting at the base of the tall palm tree; below the table glass upstand surrounded by lush planting; and at the base of the wall, to uplight the benches and sways of tall bamboos as well as the arching grasses on top of the wall. The two tonal layers of light combine to bathe the space in a purple glow that perfectly complements the round heads of the alliums, the grey leaves of the yuccas, and the magnificent agave.

By highlighting the formal box (*Buxus*) hedges, topiary, and dense planting around this dining area, a sense of privacy and comfort has been invoked, and this has been reinforced by the warm glow of the terracotta paving. Path lights beckon the onlooker into the darkened garden beyond the dining area.

In this narrow town garden, uplighters emphasize the rhythm and height of the dark sculpted trunks of standard grape vines evenly spaced along the wall. This effect has been achieved by concealing spike lights behind the luxuriant mass of lavender in full bloom.

The owners of this imposing house announce its presence by paying homage to its recently restored architecture. Powerful lamps are recessed at the base of the walls to wash the pale stonework and the intricate brickwork all the way to the roof, creating intriguing patterns and shadows. All the walls around the property are similarly bathed with light, to accentuate the structure of the garden. In the front garden, a young liquidambar is transformed into a spectacular beacon by a high-voltage uplighter.

The extraordinary work that has gone into pruning this multistemmed *Pinus sylvestris* into a cloud of pompoms had to be given full-star lighting treatment. At night, the square carpet of clipped box framing it is left in the dark, with only the tips of the tiny box leaves catching the illuminations. The wide beam of a single spike light silhouettes the whole tree, from the bare golden trunks to the pompoms, which appear feathery and unreal against the partially dark background and the lit-up arching grasses behind.

Bamboos are much loved by urban garden designers, as their height gives instant impact, their strong lines fit in wonderfully with modern schemes, and their rustling leaves are evocative of far-away forests. The row of bamboos (*Phyllostachys nigra*) planted here against a white rendered wall in a narrow town garden performs all these functions. Small spotlights have been placed at their bases, enhancing their shiny black stems and well-shaped leaves, while generating shadows on the wall behind for added interest and decoration.

RIGHT The designer of this newly planted garden was confident of the final effect when positioning a spike light in the bare soil of this border. The fitting is now completely hidden among the profuse growth of the bright yellow *Rudbeckia fulgida* var. *sullivantii* 'Goldsturm' and the tall arching grass *Miscanthus sinensis* 'Morning Light'. The light is refracted through the plants to end in tiny specks on the leaves of the cushion of box.

This spectacular banana palm (*Musa*) certainly deserves the spotlight, especially when this tropical plant has managed to flourish in the comparative cold of a London garden. A spike light has been placed at the base, to highlight the huge leaves and new shoots. It is cleverly hidden by an underplanting of soft grasses. As dusk falls, the bright red busy Lizzies (*Impatiens*) glow in the reflected light, and the cut-out leaf shapes of another great palm, *Trachycarpus fortunei*, are strikingly outlined to complete the exotic scheme.

RIGHT The star of the display here is the large tree fern (*Dicksonia antarctica*) lit from every angle, so that the wonderful geometry of its crown can be admired from the house. "Eyelid" step lights project beams across the granite setts to show off their texture and circular pattern. Copper twig-lights in the background mark a route along which to explore; in this case, the path leads to the banks of the River Thames in London.

A change of level between the paving and the timber deck has been marked out by small LED step lights in this corner of a large London roof terrace. Fibreglass containers with a metal finish have been planted with lustrous photinia along one boundary wall, and the other wall has been clad with cedar slats softened by the feathery leaves of a tamarix. Uplighting the two walls has reinforced the feeling of height and seclusion in this sitting area, while the reflections off the planters highlight the colour scheme of pale purple petunias underplanting a phormium and trachycarpus in large, pale green and purple ceramic pots.

LEFT The corner of this decked terrace could have been a difficult space to design successfully, but the combination of lighting and dramatic planting has transformed it into a focal point. The magnificent Chinese larch (*Pseudolarix*) in a ceramic pot is lit from below by a spotlight set among scattered stones and boulders. The geometric alignment of large zinc containers planted with espaliered apple trees is complemented by a further row of pots planted with box, set on top of the wall. A directional multispotlight fixed to the building throws strong shadows onto the wall, yet at the same time bathes it in a golden light, which is also softly reflected on the metal planters.

ornaments

As a garden becomes more established, ornaments may be introduced that reflect the taste, travels, or current passion of their owners. Whether a piece of sculpture is specially commissioned or comprises some extraordinary object found in a junk shop, it is important to use it in a way that fits comfortably with the original garden design and does not overcrowd the space.

A sculpture or work of art is meant to be seen to its best advantage, so should therefore be carefully sited at the end of a vista, on a plinth, or on a wall. At night it should be positioned in a spotlight, whether it is to be admired from inside the house or during a nocturnal promenade.

When a designer is planning the lighting of an ornament, its shape and style should guide the placing of the fitting: light from above will highlight the object in a theatrical way, especially if everything around it is left in the dark; light from below will pick up any jutting features and enhance textures; while light face-on will play with reflections and volumes. However, some pieces create their own light, as the fascinating sundial featured on page 128 demonstrates.

These three columns of tiered stones sit in a small pool with trickles of water constantly flowing from the top. The stones are lit up by tiny spotlights hidden just below the wall, to show off their smooth shapes and transform them into sculptures with a symbolic quality.

There is no sense of place or scale in this wonderfully abstract composition. The ball is in fact 1m (3ft) tall and made of pitted granite. It is precisely placed at the end of a stark concrete path in the axis of the main house window, and it appears to float within the sideways spotlight. The screen beyond could also be made of concrete but is in fact a wooden trellis, backlit to focus on the sharpness of the lines.

This surreal composition is lit from above by continuously glowing pink and turquoise neon strips. It is an eye-catching showcase for New Zealand artists and plants along one side of a large terrace. The crimson glass vases by Nicholas Brandon are positioned to reflect the line of light above. On the back wall among the shadows cast by the palms and native ferns, ceramic pots by Len Castle hang in a row. A salt-glaze sculpture, by Roy Cowan and looking like a plant, nestles next to the bright red blooms of the clivia. To complete the feeling of a window in a natural history museum, various animals are dotted around: seagulls by Ralph Hetzel; a wild pig by John Middleditch; and a Vietnamese elephant.

LEFT The pure lines of this cantilevered teak lounger are even more ornamental at night when lit by a powerful spotlight. This has been recessed into the terrace so that it throws a beam up the tall walls of this French château. The thin slats of the chair project dramatic shadows while acting as an impromptu screen against the glare of the lamp.

These pebbles set in cement are part of a decorative wall panel in a small enclosed courtyard, which forms a transition between house and garden. The panel, created by the garden designer, has been lit from one direction to accentuate the reflective smoothness of the pebbles and to preview the stones lining a rill in the garden beyond.

The artist Shaun Brosnan was commissioned by the owner of this London garden to make a wall fountain that would be a portrait of his father. It is made of lead worked by hand and has a reservoir at the top to let water flow over part of the face into a rill edged with grasses. Uplighters placed at the base of the rendered wall add further texture to this haunting mask, as does the hanging light in the gazebo in front.

This composition combines to perfection the elements of mystery and surprise of a classical garden, with modern lighting further enhancing the romantic atmosphere. Since it is the centrepiece of a formal knot garden, the large decorated stone urn with its box cone is strongly illustrated by a spike light hidden among the underplanting of geraniums. Such positioning helps to suggest a sense of depth and reinforces the tantalizing inaccessibility of the statue concealed in the alcove beyond.

RIGHT These antique Montpellier pots were carefully placed along the length of a raised terrace to perform several functions. Firstly, they introduce a gentle scale to the tall walls of the property and the trees in the garden beyond. Secondly, in summer, the pots are planted with orange trees, which are in harmony with the green pots and add a precious element of colour to the rather austere stone all around. Thirdly, when the terrace is illuminated for evening entertainment, the plants and the reflections in the glaze conjure a reassuring visual barrier against the darkened garden immediately below – whether or not the eye focuses on the features highlighted farther away.

This striking sculpture by Martin and Dowling has been carved out of oak and burnt with a flame to reveal the wonderful striations evocative of stacked stones and wrapped fabric. This is one of six columns, each placed on a stone plinth along both sides of a small London garden. A recessed uplighter emphasizes the texture and slender height of the sculpture against its framing of box and hornbeam.

RIGHT An extra dimension has been introduced here to the atmosphere of a London terrace by the thoughtful planning of the lighting scheme. This magnificent Buddha head set on a zinc plinth has been lit from below to accentuate the softness of the features and the downward gaze. The lighting highlights the texture of the headdress, too.

This sculpture called *Mountain Air* by Steve Dilworth could not be a better choice for this rigorously designed garden inspired by Japan. The piece is made of bronze with a glazed space in the centre containing air from the Outer Hebrides, in Scotland. It is set on a stone shelf and can only be fully seen from a grotto reached by a walk to the farthest end of the garden. In that secluded retreat, light has been kept to a minimum, and is diffused through the planting to indicate the path. It bounces off the smooth metal of this beautiful sculpture, as if to respect its enigma.

LEFT The essence of romantic gardens through the ages is represented here. This grotto sheltering the god Pan is set beyond a formal knot garden and is reached by large stepping stones above a pool. To accentuate the air of enchantment, the designer kept the lighting very soft by placing an underwater light beneath the stepping stones. Thus the wonderful statue, fountain mask, and hole stones are indirectly illuminated by reflections in the water, conjuring the feeling of a lush and damp Victorian fernery.

This full-sized replica of one of the terracotta warriors found in Xi'an, China, is now mounting guard on the terrace of a garden in Auckland. Against the backdrop of a mature cordyline lit from below to show off both its height and impressive texture, the statue is bathed in the wide beam of a small spotlight placed at ground level to form a totally striking and surreal image.

At night, the atmosphere in the same garden is quite transformed. Halogen floodlights fixed above a window opposite enhance the strength of the composition. The purple shade of the wall has been washed out by the light, which intensifies the projection of the highly polished, stainless-steel dragon, by Guy Ngan, and gives presence to the witty seagulls by Ralph Hetzel perched on top of the wall. Thus the light engenders different planes of vision to highlight the art piece and frame it with the cast shadows of branches and the carpet of the finely cut acer leaves.

The concrete wall marking the boundary of this garden in New Zealand has been painted a rich plum colour. A whole range of elements has been introduced to adorn it and maintain the southeast Asian theme – from the row of weeping acers to the stylized, metal dragon making its way along the wall.

RIGHT This abstract sculpture by the Swiss artist Gottfried Honegger is made of polished, pink granite. A single spotlight at its base celebrates its abstract shape and the different planes of the powerful image. The lighting scheme also accentuates the contrast of the hard material emerging from a cloud of purple nepeta and white roses in front of the dark green box hedge.

This rather abstract composition demonstrates yet again how lighting can glamorize the most utilitarian features, such as pipes, which are often difficult to disguise, especially at the top of a building. On this New York terrace, the large, galvanized air-conditioning pipes have deliberately not been concealed. Instead, the beam of a spotlight fixed to the nearby pergola highlights their strong shape and silvery glow against the rich orange wall dotted with the tender green of Boston ivy.

Once the sun has gone down, this sundial designed by David Harber becomes a fantastic evocation of the universe. The hand-blown glass sphere, poised on a stack of highly polished, stainless-steel disks, is lit by blue LEDs around its base to send light through the thickness of the glass and to pick up any imperfections as if they were constellations. Inside the sphere, a tiny glass ball reflects, correctly, the numbers etched in reverse on the larger ball. To project even more reflections, water moves up and down a central tube. In bringing a very modern idiom to a traditional garden ornament, artificial light has been used to take over seamlessly from natural light and provide this stunning focal point.

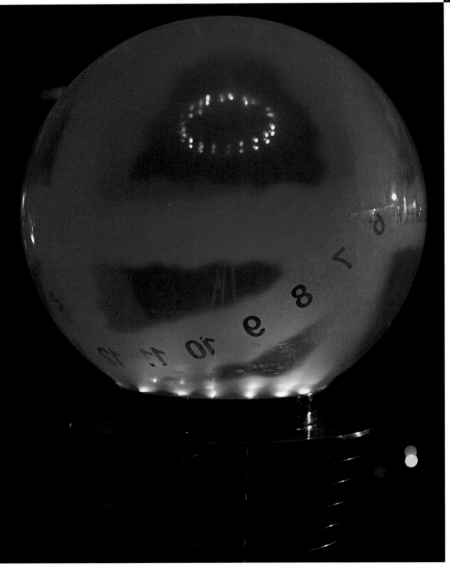

This tableau has been conceived as if it were a flower arrangement. Because the extraordinary omega-shaped light band lies among the surprising mix of white orchids and magnolia leaves, it appears like another plant form.

RIGHT Corrugated iron is not the most obvious choice of fence in a landscaped garden, yet it can be the most suitable material in some circumstances. Its reflective quality and strong vertical lines have been highlighted here by a blue LED shining through a tangle of grasses onto the scales of a copper fish designed by Nigel Cameron.

The flames of open fires, torches, and candles have always had seductive appeal. They induce warmth and a feeling of wellbeing as well as bathing faces and objects in a flattering glow. Candles add a personal touch and fit in anywhere, as they range from tiny tea-lights to tall altar candles, which will cast a timeless glow. Many sizes, colours, and scents of candles exist in between these two extremes. As the slightest breeze will extinguish a flame, candles must be displayed in containers. The possibilities are infinite – from ornate lanterns to jam jars, and from specially designed holders to storm lamps of varying sizes. It is also worth remembering that, when lighting lots of candles, a long gas lighter is more efficient and less frustrating than a box of matches.

RIGHT This enchanting creation from France is in fact a mirror framed by a coil of wire with tiny electric bulbs set in triangles of metal mesh. When hung in a tree, it would bring a fairy-tale atmosphere to any part of the garden.

In this contemporary take on the traditional lantern, a light bulb hangs inside a grey, perforated, metal tube fitted with a little weatherproof roof. The lantern, which can be suspended from a tree or a pergola, sways in the wind to produce star-shaped twinkles through the tiny holes.

With its willowy branches evoking the shape of a topiary tree, this beautiful candelabrum is eminently suitable to light up a dinner table with flair on a summer's evening. It is made of wrought-iron sprayed silver and is designed to be used with tiny candles or tea-lights set in frosted glass holders.

Alfresco meals are an important part of life on this New York roof terrace, which has been designed for easy living. In the evening, the pergola is festooned with fairy lights to create a festive atmosphere. It is also hung with a collection of variously ornate Moroccan lanterns with candles flickering through blue, gold, or pink glass. The rich red of the wall is lit up by a spotlight fixed to the house to accentuate its theatricality as a perfect backdrop for entertaining on warm summer nights.

The romantic image above was captured during an enchanted evening in a summerhouse decorated with trompe-l'oeil panels and illuminated with candles in ancient candelabra. A spellbinding atmosphere is instantly conjured up, with light bouncing softly off table settings, bottles, and carafes, embellishing everything and everyone, and leaving the rest of the world in forgotten darkness.

RIGHT This traditional music kiosk, with its raised stone floor, ornate cast-iron columns, and tiled roof has found a new purpose in a French garden. In order that it can be used for entertaining on warm summer evenings, lines of electric bulbs have been fitted among the metal vines – their light diffused by the profuse growth of a wisteria. On this particular evening, a romantic mood is produced by the simplest means: night lights in a variety of glass jars have been placed all around the raised base and on the steps to isolate the space from the rest of the garden. They have also been used to mark the kiosk entrance and have been set on the metal table in preparation for the meal to come. The warm glow of the candles is an idyllic complement to this inviting scene.

Glowing flames burning in a shallow brazier bring an instant sense of relaxation to this New York roof terrace, in spite of the very urban backdrop of office buildings. Slow-burning logs such as these make the space more comfortable as the night gets cooler. This simple and unobtrusive brazier can also be used as an efficient barbecue, in contrast to the ever-more sophisticated and imposing models that are currently popular. Now that spaces in the garden are increasingly thought of as separate rooms, open fires can be found outside too. Bonfires are not often an option because they are strictly regulated in most areas. Clay kilns with an open grate are widely available, and purpose-built outdoor fireplaces are making an interesting and welcome entrance in the world of garden design.

RIGHT Torches have been used outside for centuries to illuminate a banquet or spectacle. As such unprotected flames were considered dangerous, torches had disappeared until recently. Now they have a more controllable power supply – gas – and their stately appeal has found new favour with garden owners, as these dramatic clay beacons show. The strength of the naked flames is not only an excellent match for the metal, stone, and sword-like leaves in the garden but is also an efficient light source.

RIGHT All the decorative elements work together in this pavilion to give an exotic flavour to a meal. In their gleaming pink holders, the candles flicker and light up the Indian elephant and its rider as well as the deep pink of the orchids. The soft lighting also picks up the pink and ochre tones in the traditionally patterned tablecloth, further embellishing this carefully contrived scene.

On a sheltered terrace this simple arrangement of tea-lights in glass holders set on a square porcelain dish brings the finishing touch to a beautifully laid table. Because of the deliberate precision of the display, these otherwise traditional candles have been given an elegant and very modern twist.

This picture beautifully illustrates how a carefully designed scheme of candles combined with electrical lights results in an atmosphere of utter seduction. On this terrace in New York, the table is set under a large pergola. Billboards reveal the city beyond, yet the tall cypresses remain in the shadow and the lit-up shrubs enclose the space and create intimacy. The glamorous lighting effect is mainly produced by an intricate game of reflections. The pergola is fitted with only two downlighters, which shine on the metal table and the lustrous shells in the centre. Amber-coloured candles in tall storm lamps match the napkins and are reflected in the bottle holders, while all the lights and candles arranged in the planters nearby are also mirrored in the elegant drinking glasses, cutlery, and dark glazed bowls.

BEHIND THE SCENES

PLAYING WITH COLOUR

Now that designers are giving an increasingly important role to lighting, they are integrating it into schemes from the early stages of conception, recognizing how well-placed lights and appropriately chosen fittings will give a design the right accent.

The panoply of fittings is constantly expanding and improving, yet some old favourites such as fluorescent tubes and neon lights are making a comeback. Having been ignored for a while, they are being used again now that coloured lighting is suddenly in vogue. Inspired designers choose them mainly for urban gardens, where they are perceived as a clever way of bringing in the city lights instead of trying to compete with them.

PREVIOUS PAGES This truly magnificent group of *Dracaena draco*, with its spiky leaves, smooth patterned trunks, and underplanting of cycas, is simply lit by a single spotlight yet strongly balances the imposing water feature it faces. The contrast between nature and artifice is reinforced by the strips of neon lights that are underlining the metal frame and by the blue and red lights reflected on the stainless-steel panels hugged by sheets of water.

LEFT AND ABOVE The lighting scheme for this striking roof terrace in London's Docklands was conceived by a team comprising SOM (the architects), their landscape architect, and their lighting consultants. Following the same principles as in the building interior, they considered how to integrate the lighting into the design, how it would reinforce the landscaping, and how it would be used without being too dominant. As there were several levels on the terrace, another important factor was to highlight all hazards. The team chose fibreoptics not only to indicate a route around the space but also to introduce a party atmosphere, with the colours appearing in succession. Other advantages of fibreoptics are their very low energy consumption and the fact that the whole system originates from one location (here it is housed in the timber-clad central core), making maintenance much easier.

The circuiting is totally flexible, so that the apartment owners can select the discreet downlighters fixed to the brise-soleil or the low-voltage lights in the pool; they can also pause the colour sequence on a thin line of pink, green, yellow, or blue, or opt for all the effects at once.

LEFT Lighting has been very effectively integrated into this uncompromisingly modern garden. A narrow opening in the boundary wall houses translucent, etched glass backlit by a mint-blue fluorescent tube, to echo a fountain of the same shape on the opposite wall. A strip of blue LED lights marks the pool, accentuating its depth. Blue light bounces off the white cement render of the walls, to bathe the garden and the stunning agave in a surreal purple haze.

A wide slit in this silver-painted, concrete wall forms a spout for water to glide over and fall in a perfect sheet into a shallow pool. At night, the water and the reflection in the pool are further enhanced by a row of fibreoptic lights which are programmed to change colour every 15 seconds – from red to green, blue, then white. They can also be stopped on any colour, if desired.

neon, fluorescent light, and fibreoptics

Neon and fluorescent lights work on similar principles: a gas within a sealed glass tube is electrically charged to produce light. Neon lights in thin glass tubes were initially always red, while fluorescent tubes produced a white light. However, by perfecting the use of different gases and coatings, other colours can now be produced, making these fittings attractive to designers of contemporary gardens. As these lights make a strong statement, they are best suited to city gardens where the light level is already high and where hard landscaping prevails. In a country garden, they might be used as an art installation – such as an unexpected sign up in a tree – but they would be difficult into integrate in an overall design.

Fibreoptics probably represent the most exciting development in the world of lighting. The light of a single central lamp is "projected" through a system of mirrors along flexible glass cables to a number of points or as a continuous line, without using heat or electricity, making this type of lighting safe and economical. Fibreoptic lights have a low level of luminosity, but with their range of colours, and the fact that there are no restrictions on configurations or distances, they can produce the most wonderful displays to complement other lighting schemes.

LEDs and bespoke lights

A revolutionary type of lighting, LEDs (Light-Emitting Diodes) have only recently made a big impact, despite already being 20 years old. They provide: up to 100,000 hours of life; low voltage; very low energy consumption; no heat; and an ever-expanding range of colours. Because they use semi-conductors made of costly materials, LEDs are more expensive to buy than other forms of lighting, but in the long run they are more economical, practically maintenance free, and have the big advantage of remaining cold. They are therefore invaluable on terraces and near pools, where people might walk barefoot. Their small, durable plastic bulbs can also be incorporated in fittings made to order for specific projects.

RIGHT Because they emerge from a sea of golden day lilies, these extraordinary bespoke lights seem to evoke some slightly menacing futuristic creatures controlled by radar. Articulated, stainless-steel tubes have each been fitted with a small light bulb in a rigid cylinder at the top, to focus a precise beam of light and reinforce the disquieting effect.

This elegant light fitting is a perfect example of ingenious design. It comprises a 1-m (3-ft) long rod constructed in two parts: a solid base, which is spiked into the ground, and a clear acrylic tube along which three LED bulbs shine light. The fitting is battery operated and has a life of 200 hours. It is now mass-produced and can be bought with blue, green, or white bulbs. Because of its simplicity and versatility, allowing plants to be seen through it, this beautiful light could be used anywhere in the garden, either singly or in groups.

THE FINAL SETTING

The architecture of this modern house in New Zealand is complemented by the strong shapes of the cordylines in the front garden and by a comprehensive lighting scheme. Front gardens are often neglected, with only a light source near the door. Here the white walls and projecting roof reflect up and down scallops of light from the pillar fittings on the house, while small black bollards guide the visitor alongside the planting. Light from inside adds a diffused glow through the unadorned French windows to invite visitors inside.

Since it takes over the garden once the sun has set, artificial lighting has to compete with the daytime landscape of colours and textures effortlessly displayed in natural light. But instead of trying to match nature, the garden at night can be transformed into a place of mystery, where some features disappear and others are revealed in a totally different way: for example, the intricate structure of a tree is best seen when lit up from below; and the shape of a shrub is enhanced by a light source placed behind it. The types of fittings chosen and where they are positioned will determine the all-important mood of a garden.

In another antipodean garden, several types of lighting have been combined to illuminate structures and plants as well as to give an impression of space. By reproducing the design elements used elsewhere in the garden – such as the pierced wall – the treatment of the boundary integrates an area that could easily be overlooked, as it is farthest from the house. The concrete screen, painted purple, stands in front of white concrete panels framed by trellis. To separate the space and reinforce the illusion of depth, openings in the screens are underlined by turquoise neon lights, while the panels are lit from above by hidden spotlights to accentuate their texture and finalize the space. The elegant narrow pot and its spiky plant are also caught in the beam and provide a counterpoint to the various palm trees around the garden.

uplighters, downlighters

Garden designers were inspired by the well-tried theatrical use of footlights, and so uplighting was the first type of electrical lighting to be introduced into gardens. A feature lit from below stands out and attracts attention.

Uplighters have not lost their appeal, as there is an ever-wider choice of fittings and designs to suit most styles, requirements, and budgets. Among this panoply, spike lights remain the most popular type. A garden will always have sufficient space to insert a light into some soil – whether in the ground or in a pot – and as long as the fitting is pointing at the object to be emphasized, and away from the viewer, you have the basis of a successful lighting scheme. The size of the garden and the way in which the lighting is designed, the choice of areas and features to pinpoint, as well as vital safety considerations will determine the extent and complexity of the electrical circuit.

Downlighters have to be fixed to a wall or other structure, making sure that their beam does not blind passers-by. Fixed to a pergola, they can illuminate a dining table or climbing plants weaving their way up the posts. Downlighting from the top of a tree will create eye-catching shadows through the branches and possibly reveal a carpet of flowering bulbs underneath. Flowers are enhanced by this type of lighting, as they mainly face upwards and would not be seen if lit from below through dense planting.

Most lighting schemes use both up and downlighting. In the same area, such a combination will provide more illumination on a path or wash an interesting wall or feature, while in separate areas the design might produce rhythmic oases of light, inviting the viewer farther into the garden or drawing attention to a range of plants or a specimen tree.

The recently restored stonework of this house and garden is highlighted by recessed 20-watt lights placed at the base of the walls. The reflective quality of the pale stone does not warrant more powerful lights or excessive illumination in this country garden. It should be noted how lighting here succeeds in playing its dual role of enhancing the site and guiding the eye.

The length of this wrap-around roof terrace is both stressed and broken up by the discreet beams of overhead lights fixed to the metal brise-soleil. The owners, who have recently moved in, have installed just enough furniture to be able to sit out and enjoy the view, but will eventually make use of the lights to enhance plants in containers and further seating areas.

RIGHT Uplighters and downlighters have been used in this courtyard to produce a feeling of intimacy and wellbeing, in anticipation of the dinner to come. Candles in small glazed bowls form a centrepiece and add the final touch. An uplit magnolia in a grey clay pot screens neighbouring houses and a Buddha head to the left of the tree is lit from below, while a downlighter focuses attention on the pure lines of a clay urn.

At night, the path leading to a bridge in this garden is a light show of small acrylic cylinders, purpose-made and fitted with fibreoptic light. A colour wheel of blue, white, green, and purple has been placed on the fibreoptic "projector", enabling the colours to change in a timed sequence. Fibreoptics are invaluable in terms of introducing an element of surprise to a garden.

RIGHT In this area of a New Zealand garden, the soaring shapes of grasses and phormium, as well as their tones of blue-green and splashes of red, have been accentuated by fine jets of mist projected at intervals along tiny pipes on the ground. They are also captured by coloured halogen spotlights with blue and red bulbs that add prisms of colour through the water.

In this newly planted garden, lighting was installed from the start, on bare soil among tiny clumps of herbaceous plants. By summer, when this border is at the height of its bloom, there is a case for keeping lighting to a bare minimum or even not having any at all. However, here the shape of the grasses has been strengthened by the light from below, as has the strong yellow of the rudbeckia, although the other flowering plants seem lost in the overall tangle.

The strong beams of four underwater lights are directed at this carved stone pillar, which contains a fountain and is positioned in a large pool. The illuminations not only reveal details of the carving but also transform the water trickling from the top into a golden cloud.

RIGHT Light plays its part in this wonderful ode to recycling in a small New York courtyard. Water pours from an industrial tap fitting (found in a local café during its refurbishment) onto a portion of cast-iron gutter that was removed from the building when it was converted. The flow of water then splashes onto yellow pieces of Perspex. Decoration is provided by other found objects: a telecommunication device sits in the gutter, while a worn Italian family crest rests on the ground. The white beam of an industrial spotlight illuminates and brings together this eclectic collection, accentuating the water tumbling onto the Perspex and the reflections on the wet pebbles.

PREVIOUS PAGES A well-designed lighting scheme, using simple fittings, brings great elegance to a design. In the classical garden of this Georgian house, recessed uplighters mark out routes in the white gravel and along the colonnade, while accentuating the formality and processional sense given by the columns and the trees. A timber walkway with six recessed lights crosses the garden among symmetrical formations of clipped box. Downlighters fitted with shields are recessed in the ceiling of the covered walkway not only to guide visitors to the door but also to project scalloped shapes onto the wall and illuminate the white Buddha near the house.

Step lighting is a very important consideration in a garden in order to avoid danger as well as to transform steps into a strong sculptural element. Tiny LEDs recessed in the flank wall are a good way of doing this. Placed just above the tread, they project a short beam sideways on the surface of the riven stone without any shadow or blinding glare. Other fittings have downward louvres or an eyelid to ensure comfort and safety.

This is the classic and most commonly used recessed light fitting, with its stainless-steel finish. It uses a 20-watt halogen reflector lamp, can be fitted with a toughened-glass screen, and is set flush with the deck to avoid any tripping hazard. The finish can be shiny or matt steel, copper, or brass. The intensity of the lamp can vary, and the surround can be much narrower than this one, or square. Such fittings are an ideal starting point for lighting, and there is a large range of international products from which to choose.

Thanks to its excellent design, this "floor scan" performs a double role as a marker and as a feature in itself. It indicates the edge of a timber deck floating above a "river" of tumbled slate — or paddle stones — while diffusing a gentle light on the different materials. The soft grey of the matt finish is in total harmony with the slate and the band of pale grey stone on the other side. Such a fitting appears in many manufacturers' catalogues, which display a huge range of designs and are certainly worth requesting.

underwater lights, lighting water

As water is now an almost essential feature of many gardens, finding ways of lighting it has become an equally important part of the design. If it is to be lit from below, water has to be clear. Swimming pools and other basins tiled or painted in pale colours will benefit from lights recessed in the sides, as the blue mass of water and its endless refractions take on a magical quality. Underwater lights can also point at a fountain above the water, an ornament standing on the edge, or planting surrounding the pool. However, natural ponds or pools lined with butyl will not be enhanced by underwater lights, because folds of the lining or the cloudiness of the water will be revealed, and plants will be concealed.

The reflective power of water is also a huge asset when, instead of the water itself being lit, illumination is directed onto striking features nearby, such as a tree or an eye-catching building to be perfectly mirrored in the still surface of a dark pool.

This water composition forms the top of a cube placed between planters in the corner of a large roof terrace. A smooth sheet of slate has been pierced with nine holes, through which water bubbles and runs over the slate into a very thin slit. The shadow-line effect is complemented by the lights underneath the water, to reinforce further the contrasts of light–dark and dry–wet.

LEFT This ambitious man-made cascade tumbling over two pools in a garden in Kent, England, has made discreet but effective use of lighting with only two fittings. One under water light has been placed at the base of the taller cascade, to create a glimmering effect on the wet rough stone. Although the fitting is hidden by the turbulence, the diffused beam reinforces the height and movement of the sheet of water. The other light beam is more visible, being positioned under a stone bridge crossing a gentler cascade. The golden glow highlights the stillness of the pool under the bridge, making it more inviting and safer to cross.

RIGHT This wall light uses a 50-watt, low-voltage halogen bulb with a transformer incorporated into the rectangular box behind. The brushed aluminium finish has been well chosen to harmonize with the zinc plinth and the grey of the simple clay urn. The beam encompasses the urn shape but subtly leaves the base in shadow, and, with its downwards scallop of light, distracts attention from the height of the wall.

This bespoke, galvanized wall sconce is one of a pair set either side of French windows leading onto a roof terrace. Not only is the sharp design in keeping with the contemporary style of the terrace but also, because of the highly reflective metal used inside, the luminaires provide a good level of light. They act as downlighters for the specimen plants below and throw light onto the walls of the building, reinforcing the boundaries of this exposed space and adding a feeling of intimacy. As they are on a separate switch operated from inside, the lights can be turned off altogether when the owners choose to dine only by candlelight and the distant city illuminations.

floodlights, security lights

Floodlighting is the ultimate lighting technique and has long been used in order to emblazon historic monuments. It has therefore given rise to the very popular spectacles of "Son et Lumière", in which ancient ruins are brought to life by a combination of storytelling, music, and light. Floodlights aim to imitate daylight, using powerful lamps – up to 500 watt – to wash over whole areas, either from above or below, with uniform intensity and little subtlety. This works well over large areas where a big impact or a sense of occasion are needed, although unacceptably high levels of light pollution are not welcomed by neighbours or nocturnal creatures.

Security lights are floodlights fixed to a house in order to deter intruders. They can be triggered by infrared movement sensors or fitted with a timer. While it has not been proven that a sudden burst of light is an effective deterrent, security lights do make some homeowners feel safer. However, they must be installed on a separate circuit to that of the general atmospheric garden lighting and be switched on only when required.

The security lights have come on in this garden. Surprisingly, because this is high summer, when the borders are bursting with strong colours and shapes, the harsh light directed from above enhances the profusion of plants instead of overwhelming it. It is probably a good idea to light up such a barrier of planting in front of the house, because it could easily be used as a hiding place for burglars.

RIGHT Floodlights have been used to light up this extraordinary front garden, which is still quite new so the climbers have not yet covered all the structures. Small 100-watt halogen lamps have been fitted at the apex of each of the metal arbours, which are made of reinforcing rods. The lighting works well as it has been designed to show off leaf shapes and flowers from above, as well as to accentuate the four planting beds and the paths. Even though the light level is high, it does not disturb neighbouring houses, because all the lamps point downwards.

This small fitting hung from the branch of a
birch tree on a roof terrace in New York boldly
demonstrates how lighting conjures up different
planes of vision as well as defining space. When
pitched against the grid of lit-up windows in the
skyscraper beyond, the regular perforations on
the metal lantern accentuate in the most
startling fashion the contrast between finite
private garden and vast public surroundings.

Employing a lighting designer

Installing a lighting scheme, even if it only involves two or three fittings, is best left to the professionals.

If your outside space is an important part of your life, not only for entertaining and pure enjoyment but also to be seen from the house, then it is almost imperative to have a well-thought-out lighting scheme.

You might think that employing a lighting designer is expensive but some do not charge a separate fee and will design a scheme as part of a package, including the supply of fittings. Designers are also able to advise on the ever-increasing range of products and the latest developments in lighting, as well as having access to specialist outlets.

Recommendation is always a good route and so is the Internet as it enables you to see completed schemes and detailed effects.

If you decide to employ a consultant, who will most probably be charging on an hourly basis, be well prepared and know exactly what you and everyone using the garden expect from the space. You might only ask the consultant to draw up a plan that is then handed over to an electrician. If you ask them to supervise the work all the way through, the charge is likely to be a percentage of the cost of the job.

Employing an electrician

In many countries it is actually illegal for anyone other than a qualified electrician to carry out any electrical work outside a house. Rules and regulations have become very stringent as electricity outside implies possible exposure to water through corrosion; it also might involve high voltage and possible contact with timber, which in turn may involve fire risks.

Again, rely on recommendations, although be sure to use an electrician with the right qualifications – many electricians have no experience of working with outdoor lighting.

Be very clear about your requirements and do not feel you have to accept the products the electrician is used to.

It will be easy to work out the layout of a lighting scheme and install the cables in a newly landscaped garden. In an established garden, some of the cabling might not be totally concealed although it should be kept to the perimeter of the spaces as much as possible using black conduits.

Armoured cables must be laid deeply enough to avoid any accident and if that is not possible because of existing conditions, they must be further protected within suitable ducts.

Another important consideration is to keep the outdoor circuit totally separate from the interior one even though the switches will probably be inside. You do not want a faulty garden light to trip the house circuit.

Finally, and you should be able to rely on your electrician for this, make sure the adequate power supply is allocated to the exterior scheme as it might involve pumps, irrigation systems, and pool equipment besides garden lights.

Choosing the lights

However you decide to organize the work, you will most probably want to be involved in the choice of fittings. If time is short, the Internet will give you instant information. You can also send for catalogues. These are usually beautifully produced and feature mouth-watering schemes and effects.

But if you have a little more time, the most enjoyable way is to look at products at garden shows. You will be able to see many stands set up to seduce and inspire. More and more show gardens include lighting and even though you might not be able to appreciate the full effect in daylight, you can see the fittings and talk to the designers. Lighting product stands will have specialists on hand for demonstration of all the various fittings, and advice on what would be best suited to your needs. You may well leave a show not only laden with catalogues but having also bought a set of extraordinary fairy lights or an amazing lantern.

plants 88–109
  downlighting *166*
  spotlighting *50, 54, 68, 88, 90–1, 94–7, 104, 144*
  uplighting *64, 88, 100, 154, 156*
potagers *9, 54, 64*

R

recessed lighting
  on decking *90, 163*
  in floor surfaces 62, *67*
  for paths *9, 22, 33, 162*
  spotlights *39*
  on steps *42,* 62, *162*
  swimming pools 165
  in walls 62, *152*
reflections *29, 44, 50–1, 57, 76, 87, 92, 128 see also* mirrors
roof terraces
  candlelit *23, 36, 134*
  directional lighting *27*
  downlighting *39, 154*
  fibreoptic lights *17, 145*
  interior lighting *27*
  lanterns *23, 27, 134, 170*
  LED lights *109*
  spotlighting *23, 27, 36, 134*
  underwater lighting *43*
  uplighting *23, 39, 109*
rope lights *64*

S

safety issues
  of lighting installation 62, *172–3*
  lighting's role *11,* 38, *40, 43,* 62–5, *71, 145, 162–3*
  security lights 168
screens *22, 44, 151*
SOM *145*
spike lights *9, 78, 83, 95, 102, 104, 106,* 152
spotlighting 9, *47*

dining areas *36*
ornaments *110–11, 115, 126*
planters *116*
plants *50, 54, 68, 88, 90–1, 94–7, 104, 144*
swimming pools *39*
trees *9, 15, 27, 47, 67, 88, 92–3, 106*
walls *54, 57, 60, 109, 134, 151*
stepping stones 62, *68*
steps *11, 42, 47, 62–3, 67, 68, 106, 162*
storm lamps *23, 36*
strip lighting *33, 60, 63, 64, 100, 113*
sunsets *9, 12, 17*
Surrey, England *54*
swimming pools *15, 17, 22, 38–43, 67*

T

tea-lights *18, 39,* 130, *134, 138*
terraces *11, 35, 54, 116, 141 see also* roof terraces
torches *136*
trees *9, 60,* 88–109
  downlighting 88, 152
  floodlighting *13*
  natural lighting *12*
  spotlighting *9, 15, 27, 47, 67, 88, 92–3, 106*
  uplighting *9, 22, 39, 67, 72, 101–2, 109,* 150
twig-lights *9, 26, 106*

U

underwater lighting 165
  in swimming pools *15, 17, 40, 43*
  in water features *26, 44–5, 74–6, 78–81, 84, 158, 165*
uplighting 152–63
ceilings *40*
ornaments *67, 118, 123, 154*
pergolas *54*
planters *23, 35, 109*
plants *68, 84, 100, 154, 156*

trees *9, 22, 39, 67, 72, 101–2, 109,* 150
walls *10, 33, 102, 109, 150, 152*
water features *47, 54, 57, 77, 81, 95, 115, 158*
see also underwater lighting

V

visual effects 44–57, *60, 145,* 147, 170

W

walls 51, 60
  downlighting *50, 150, 166*
  pillar lights *11, 26, 150*
  spotlighting *54, 57, 60, 109, 134, 151*
  uplighting *10, 33, 102, 109, 150, 152*
  wall lights *28, 54, 67*
  wall sconces *27, 166*
water features 57, 74–87
  cascades *77, 78, 84, 147, 158, 165*
  downlighting *158, 165*
  fountains 22–3, *47, 74, 76, 81, 83, 115, 158*
  ponds *54,* 95
  pools *26, 44–5, 50-1, 78, 83, 87, 92, 100*
  underwater lighting *26, 44–5, 74–6, 78–81, 84, 158, 165*
  uplighting *47, 54, 57, 77, 81, 95, 115, 158*
  see also swimming pools

AUTHOR'S ACKNOWLEDGMENTS

I would like to thank Michèle Byam and Sarah Rock who believed in the idea and helped produce such a beautiful book. I also thank Joanna Chisholm, who edited the text with the lightest touch. Writing this book has been a most enjoyable experience.

I have to thank all the garden owners who opened their doors with such enthusiasm late at night and in particular Bill and Anne Dickson; Roy Simpson; Joanna Prentice; Caroline and Malcolm Thorb, Alain-Dominique Perrin, Ballymore, Sandro Marpillero and Linda Pollak, Tim and Dagny duVal.

For their time and generosity in revealing their professional secrets, or pointing me in the right direction, I am extremely grateful to the following designers:

In England:
Sarah Roberts at John Cullen
John Wyer: pp.11, p67, 69, 78, 90, 106, 108, 109, 165
David Haselhurst: pp.13, 42, 79, 96, 100, 103, 107, 110, 152–53, 164, 168
Jeroen van Raalte, pp.70–1, 91, 97
Bill Dickson, with Mary Greenhalgh at John Cullen, and Matt Baxter at Tsutaya: pp.46–7, 86–7, 120–21
Luciano Giubbelei: pp.2, 30–1, 34–5, 39, 66, 118, 119, 138, 155, 160–61, 167
Laara Copley-Smith: pp.9, 24–5, 32, 102, 105, 115, 156b
Philip Nash: front cover, pp.98–9, 146
Johnston Bourne: pp.84, 89
Phil Jaffa with Tony Cradoch at Poulsen: pp.85, 88
Claire Mee: p.33, with Roy Simpson pp.56–7, 68, 75, 101, 104
David Harber: p.128
Simon Scott at Haddonstone: pp.1, 116, 122
Erik de Maeijer and Jane Hudson: pp.83, 94

Ian Braines at Haley Somerset with SOM: pp.16, 17, 63, 65, 144, 145, 154
Joan Clifton at Avant-Garden: pp.130r, 131
Conran: p.148
p.64 original design by Future System with DPL

In New-Zealand:
Nigel Cameron: pp.10, 28, 76, 115, 128tr, 129, 149, 150, 156t, 157
Ron Sang: pp.50, 112–13, 123, 124, 125
Ted Smythe: pp.20–1, 60, 142–43, 151
Dan Rutherford at Sphere: p.61
Cilla Cooper: pp.44–5, 147

In New York:
Tim and Dagny duVal: back cover, pp.12, 22, 23, 82, 130, 140–41
Philip Roche at Plant Specialists, Inc: pp.26, 27, 36–7, 43, 55, 166, 170–71
Rebecca Loncraine:pp.126, 132–33, 136
Marpillero Pollak Architects: pp.29, 48-9, 76br, 77, 159
I would also like to thank Bill Saunders and François de Ménil for inspired introductions.

My own work is featured on pp.6, 38, 40–1, 52–3, 72–3, 93, 127, 135, 163
Thanks to Serge for the wonderful effect on pp.58–9.

Further reading:
Garden Lighting by John Raine
The Lighting Book by Deyan Sudjic

And, of course, huge thanks to Steve for such wonderful pictures, and Edward for his gentle help.